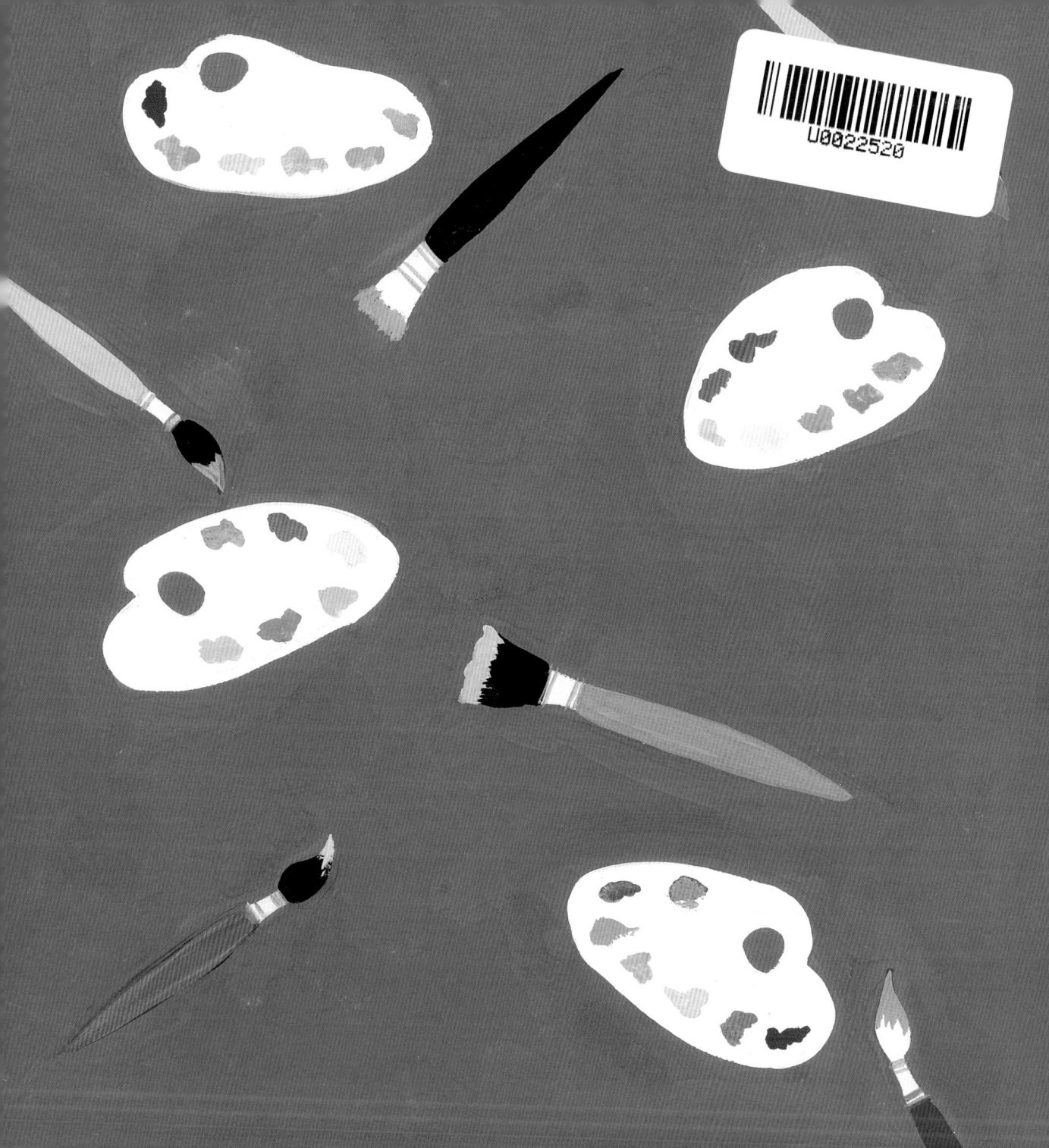

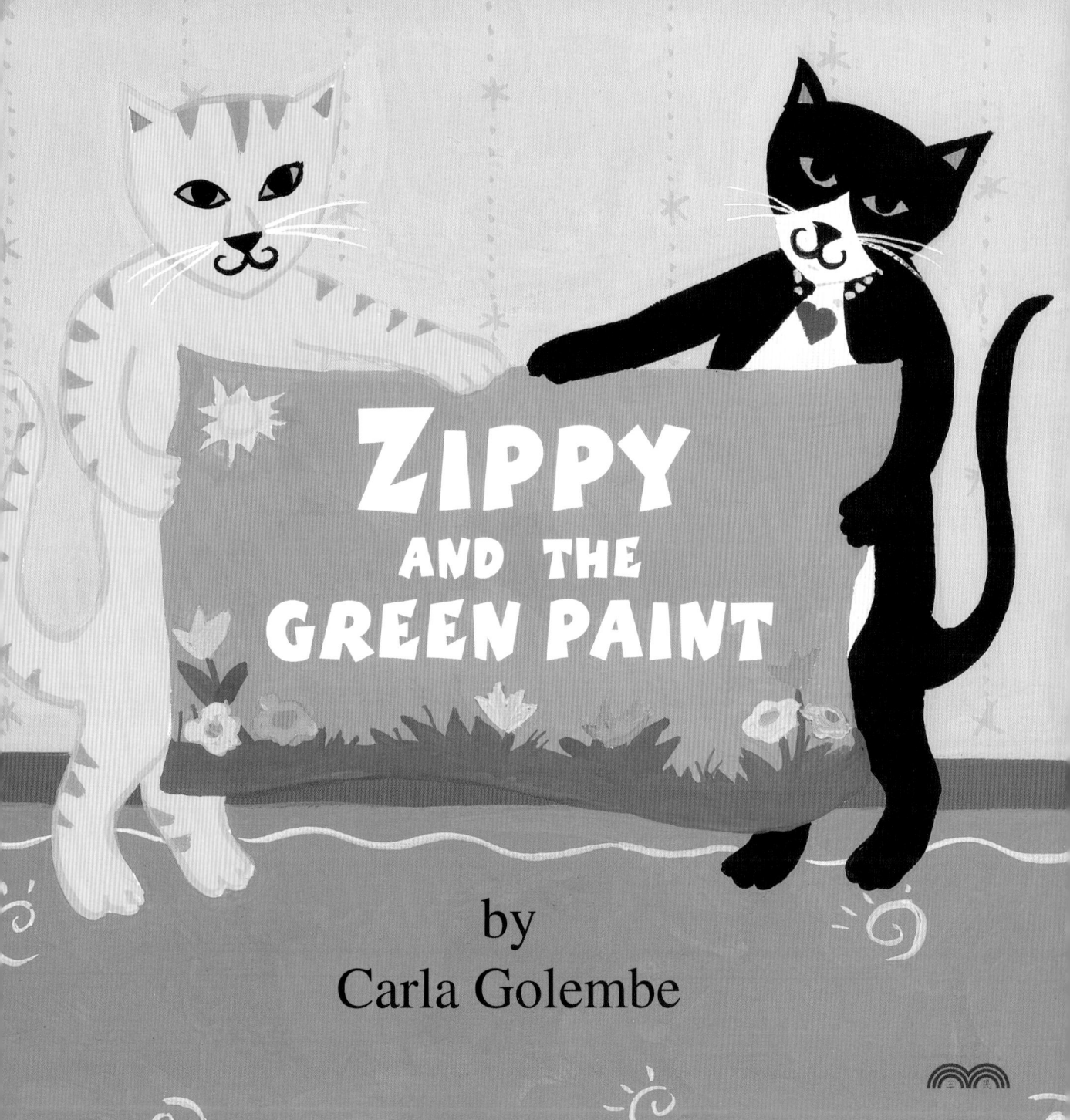

ZIPPY
AND THE
GREEN PAINT

by

Carla Golembe

He paints trees and flowers.

He paints pictures of cats.

Sometimes he paints *mice.

Zippy wants to make a birthday card for Zoe.

So he gets out his paper.

He gets out his brushes.
He gets out his paints.

He paints the sky blue.

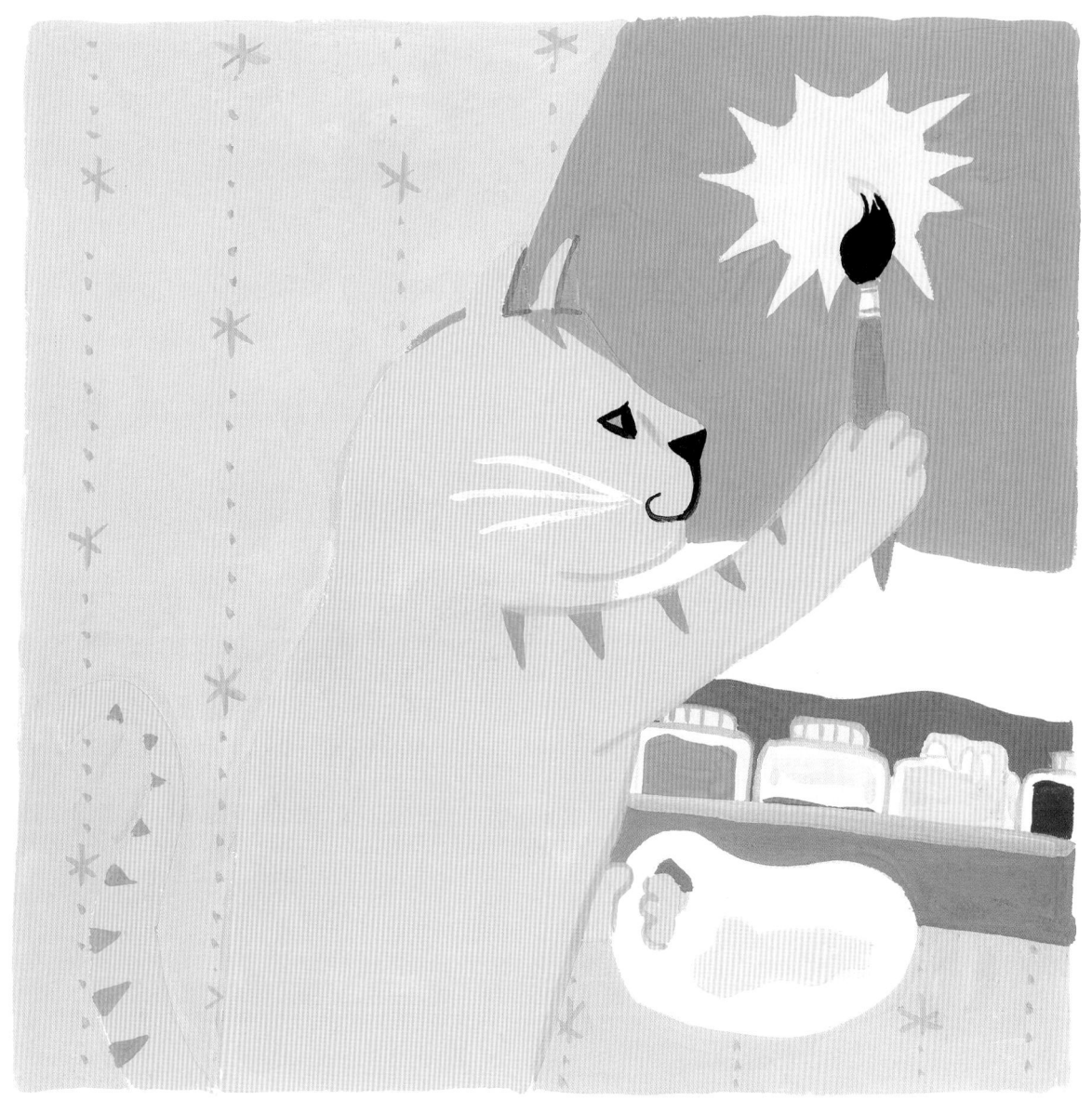

He paints the sun yellow.

He paints some flowers red.

He wants to paint the grass green.

12

But when he opens the *jar of green paint, it is *empty.
"Oh-oh," says Zippy.

He runs to the store to buy some green paint,
but the store is closed.

"Oh no!" cries Zippy.

Zippy feels sad as he walks home. What will he do?

Will he have to paint the grass yellow, red or blue?

Zippy *dips his brush in the blue paint.
*Splat! Some blue falls into the yellow.
"Oops!" says Zippy.

He tries to get the blue paint out of the yellow, but the colors get mixed up. He tries again and they mix some more.

They mix and mix until all the paint turns green.

"Wow!" *shouts Zippy.

19

Zippy paints the grass green.

He is very excited about making green.

He decides to see what other colors he can make.

He mixes red and yellow together and makes orange.

So Zippy makes a card for Zoe with all the colors of the rainbow. He gives it to Zoe for her birthday.

Zoe says, "This is the most beautiful card I've ever seen." She
*hangs it above the couch. And everyone who sees it loves
Zippy's painting.

p.10

他將天空塗上藍色，

p.11

將太陽塗上黃色，

p.12

還將一些花朵塗上紅色。
他想把草地塗上綠色，

p.13

但是當他打開綠色顏料的罐子時，裡面竟然是空的！
賽皮說：「糟了！」

p.14-15

他跑去商店買綠色的顏料，可是店卻沒有開。
賽皮大叫：「喔，不！」

p.16

賽皮傷心的走回家。他該怎麼辦呢？難道他要將草地塗成黃色、紅色或藍色的嗎？

♥ *p.17*

賽皮拿畫筆沾了沾藍色的顏料。「啪!」的一聲,一些藍色顏料滴進黃色顏料裡了。
賽皮說:「唉唷!」

✹ *p.18*

他試著把藍色顏料從黃色顏料裡弄出來,但這兩種顏色卻混在一起;他又試了一次,結果它們混得更徹底了。

♥ *p.19*

這兩種顏料就這樣不斷的混合,最後全部變成了綠色。
賽皮高興的大喊:「哇!」

✹ *p.20*

於是,賽皮將草地塗上了綠色。能夠製造出綠色來,他覺得好興奮喔!

♥ *p.21*

所以,他決定試試看他還能混合出哪些顏色。
他把紅色跟黃色混合在一起,變成了橘色。

💜 *p.22*

他把紅色跟藍色混合在一起，變成了紫色。

☀ *p.23*

他把紅色跟白色混合在一起，變成了粉紅色。
賽皮驚訝的大喊：「好酷喔！」

💜 *p.24*

後來，賽皮用彩虹的七種顏色畫了一張卡片，
送給柔依作為生日禮物。

☀ *p.25*

柔依說：「這是我看過最漂亮的卡片了！」她把這
張卡片掛在沙發上方。每個看到的人都很喜歡
賽皮的作品呢！

調色盤的配色法：

灰色 (grey) ＝ 黑色 (black) ＋ 白色 (white)

咖啡色 (brown) ＝ 紅色 (red) ＋ 綠色 (green)

粉紅色 (pink) ＝ 紅色 (red) ＋ 白色 (white)

淺紫色 (light purple) ＝ 紫色 (purple) ＋ 白色 (white)

＝ 紅色 (red) ＋ 藍色 (blue) ＋ 白色 (white)

色彩的世界

在「賽皮與綠色顏料」故事中，賽皮發現原來顏色是可以被混合出來的！下面我們就來學習一些關於顏色的事情。

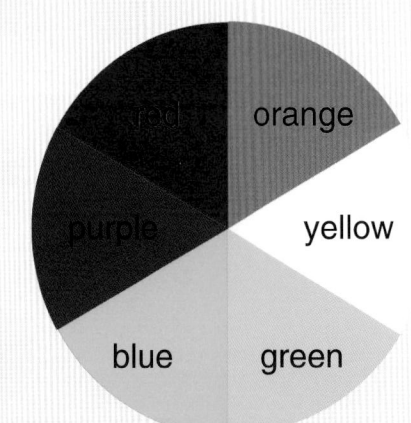

Part. 1　認識色輪 (color wheel)

色輪是由六塊扇形組合而成的，表示顏色跟顏色之間的關係。

紅色、黃色、藍色被叫做「自然界的三原色」，這三種顏色是不能用別的顏色混合出來的。

那麼另外三種顏色——橘色、綠色、紫色是怎麼來的呢？仔細觀察下面的圖，再看看色輪，你就會知道答案了！

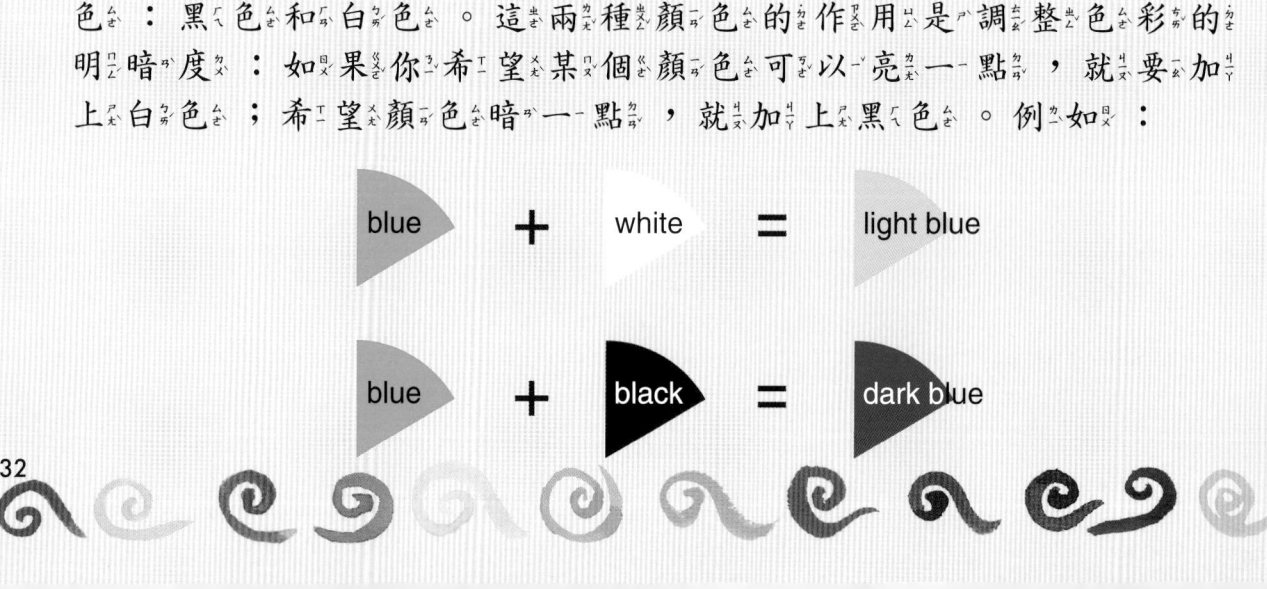

你發現了嗎？在色輪上，橘色、綠色和紫色其實是由相鄰的兩種顏色混合而成的喔！

另外，有兩種沒有出現在色輪上，卻很重要的顏色：黑色和白色。這兩種顏色的作用是調整色彩的明暗度：如果你希望某個顏色可以亮一點，就要加上白色；希望顏色暗一點，就加上黑色。例如：

Part. 2 小朋友，輪到你來動動腦嘍！猜猜看下面的顏色，各是由什麼顏色混合出來的呢？

（正確答案在第 30 頁喔！）

grey = _____ + _____

brown = _____ + _____

pink = _____ + _____

light purple = _____ + _____

Author's Note

Writers get ideas for stories from many things. The idea for "Zippy and the Green Paint" comes from my cats and from my students. Zippy and Zoe are my cats. They are best friends. They are very smart and cute.

I teach art to college students. One of the classes I teach is called "Color Theory." The students learn everything about color. They paint color wheels. They learn to mix one hundred colors! The first color they learn to mix is green.

作者的話

作家會從很多東西得到故事的靈感。「賽皮與綠色顏料」這個故事的想法，來自於我的貓和我的學生們。賽皮與柔依是我養的貓，牠們是最要好的朋友，非常聰明可愛。

我在大學教美術，我上的其中一門課叫做「色彩理論」。學生們在這堂課中學習關於顏色的所有事情；他們要畫色輪，還要學會混合出一百種顏色呢！他們第一個學習混合的顏色就是綠色。

About the Author

Carla Golembe is the illustrator of thirteen children's books, five of which she wrote. Carla has won several awards including a New York Times Best Illustrated Picture Book Award. She has also received illustration awards from Parents' Choice and the American Folklore Society. She has twenty-five years of college teaching experience and, for the last thirteen years, has given speaker presentations and workshops to elementary schools. She lives in Southeast Florida, with her husband Joe and her cats Zippy and Zoe.

關於作者

Carla Golembe 擔任過十三本童書的繪者，其中五本是由她寫作的。Carla 曾多次獲獎，包括《紐約時報》最佳圖畫書獎。她也曾獲全美父母首選基金會，以及美國民俗學會的插畫獎項。她有二十五年的大學教學經驗，而在過去的十三年中，曾經在多所小學中演講及舉辦研討會。她目前和丈夫 Joe 以及她的貓——賽皮與柔依，住在美國佛羅里達州東南部。

賽皮與柔依系列
ZIPPY AND ZOE SERIES

想知道我們發生了什麼驚奇又爆笑的事嗎？
歡迎學習英文0-2年的小朋友一起來分享我們的故事 ——
「賽皮與柔依系列」，讓你在一連串有趣的事情中學英文！

精裝／附中英雙語朗讀CD／全套六本

Carla Golembe 著／繪

本局編輯部 譯

Hello！我是賽皮，我喜歡畫畫、做餅乾，還有跟柔依一起去海邊玩。偷偷告訴你們一個秘密：我在馬戲團表演過喔！

Hi，我是柔依，今年最開心的事，就是賽皮送我一張他親手畫的生日卡片！賽皮是我最要好的朋友，他很聰明也很可愛，我們兩個常常一起出去玩！

賽皮與柔依系列有

1 賽皮與綠色顏料
(Zippy and the Green Paint)

2 賽皮與馬戲團
(Zippy and the Circus)

3 賽皮與超級大餅乾
(Zippy and the Very Big Cookie)

4 賽皮做運動
(Zippy Chooses a Sport)

5 賽皮學認字
(Zippy Reads)

6 賽皮與柔依去海邊
(Zippy and Zoe Go to the Beach)

國家圖書館出版品預行編目資料

Zippy and the Green Paint:賽皮與綠色顏料 / Carla
Golembe著;Carla Golembe繪;本局編輯部譯.－
－初版一刷.－－臺北市：三民，2006
　　面；　　公分.－－(Fun心讀雙語叢書.賽皮與柔
　　依系列)
中英對照
ISBN 957－14－4450－2　　(精裝)

1.英國語言－讀本

523.38　　　　　　　　　　　　94026564

網路書店位址　http://www.sanmin.com.tw

© **Zippy and the Green Paint**
—— 賽皮與綠色顏料

著作人　Carla Golembe
繪　者　Carla Golembe
譯　者　本局編輯部
發行人　劉振強
著作財　三民書局股份有限公司
產權人　臺北市復興北路386號
發行所　三民書局股份有限公司
　　　　地址 / 臺北市復興北路386號
　　　　電話 / (02)25006600
　　　　郵撥 / 0009998－5
印刷所　三民書局股份有限公司
門市部　復北店 / 臺北市復興北路386號
　　　　重南店 / 臺北市重慶南路一段61號
初版一刷　2006年1月
編　號　S 806171
定　價　新臺幣壹佰捌拾元整
行政院新聞局登記證局版臺業字第○二○○號

有著作權　不准侵害

ISBN　957－14－4450－2　　(精裝)

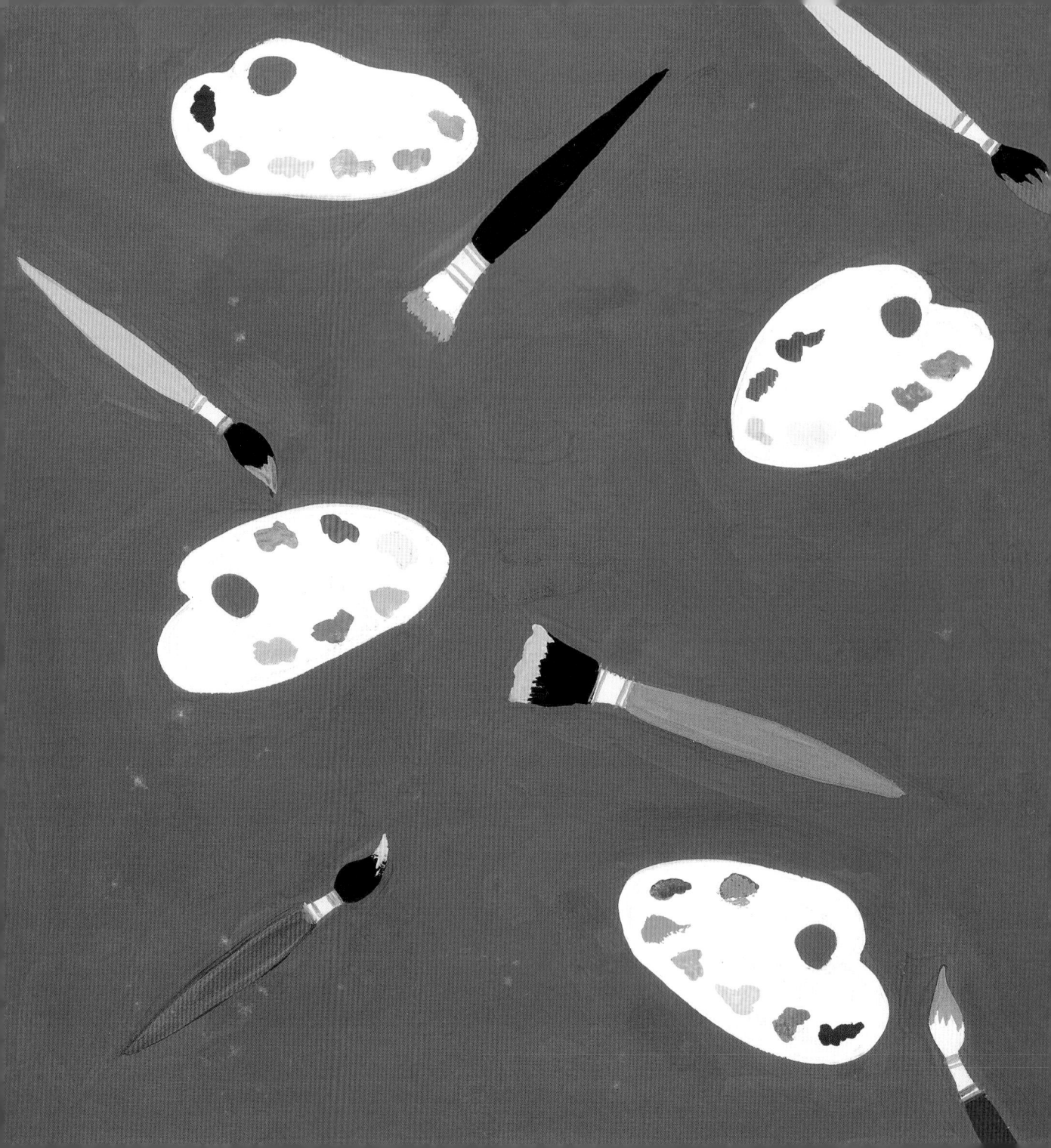